Other books by Erica

Praying is (not) Hard

Holy Doubt

A 28-DAY DEVOTIONAL JOURNEY TO
UNWRAP THE WONDER OF CHRISTMAS

Fulfilled

Erica Barthalow

Fulfilled
© 2023 Erica Barthalow

Cover and interior design by KUHN Design Group | kuhndesigngroup.com
Author photo by Seneca Epley

ISBN (Hardcover) 978-0-9989953-8-0

ISBN (Paperback) 979-8-9914503-0-0

ISBN (Epub) October 2023 978-0-9989953-9-7

Printed in the United States of America

For my mom,
who was the first to introduce me to
the wonder of Christmas

Contents

Week Four: Prepare & Receive

Week One

CONNECTING

ONE

Presence over Presents

*"In your presence is fullness of joy; in your right
hand there are pleasures forevermore."*

PSALM 16:11

Stepping into the chaos of what my husband affectionately (or perhaps not so affectionately) refers to as the "Christmas crud" in our basement storage room to slide yet another plastic tote on the shelf, I was swallowed by a sense of sadness. The season had passed and it would be a whole year before it would be culturally acceptable to listen to Christmas music again (a decidedly depressing fact for an extreme lover of Christmas like myself), but this sadness was laced with something more.

Every year on December 26th (sometimes even on the 25th), I look around at the crumpled gift wrap, the empty boxes, and I feel a familiar ache.

This ache says I've missed it. The season has come, and now gone, to celebrate and savor the birth of my Savior and I haven't done it well. I've gotten carried away in meaningless pursuits, more cookies to bake, more shopping to do, the list goes on and on. The Christmas season happened *to* me instead of happening *in* me. Maybe you've felt this too? Perhaps you've been so caught up in the busyness of the season that you forgot to revel in what it's really all about.

Ultimately, I realized I settled for:

* Consuming over connecting

* Weariness over wonder

* Traditions over transformation

Something needed to change. I was hungry to be fulfilled by Christ alone. My soul begged for a different approach to the season as I entered the chaos of that Christmas storage room. In short, I had settled for "a thimble when God has nothing less to give ... than the ocean of himself."[1] The title of this book is *Fulfilled,* and it's ironic because honestly, by the time that Christmas season came to a close, I felt anything but fulfilled. I was frantic and feeling less connected to Jesus than I had before the season began. Stuffing everything back onto the shelf for one more year and closing the door, I vowed that next year would be different.

We can't control the amount of parties we're invited to, or the amount of cookies that beg to be baked, or any number of things that want to crowd our schedules and our souls during the Christmas season, but we can control our yes. We can choose to thoughtfully and prayerfully cultivate a season that allows us time to sit in wonder and truly behold the beauty of a God who would deign to dwell with us. Emmanuel. He came, and he is here still.

In this season where it's easy to be consumed with trying to find fulfillment in more, more, more, my prayer is that the words on these pages bring you back to the One who will provide true fulfillment and contentment in this, and every, season.

Pause & Reflect

Of the list above, which item are you most likely to settle for this Advent season? What is one way that you can actively and purposefully fight against it in your life?

TWO

Confessions

"And I will cause hostility between you and the woman,
and between your offspring and her offspring. He will
strike your head, and you will strike his heel."

GENESIS 3:15

When your mind wanders to Christmas and you think of words to describe the season, what comes to mind? If you're like me, I naturally think of things like decorating the Christmas tree, the smell of cinnamon rolls baking, or the gentle refrain of familiar and new Christmas songs filling the air. Your mind probably doesn't immediately go to repentance or confession. I'd venture to say we don't often associate Christmas with our sinful condition, but it was the reason Jesus came to us.

The Christmas story didn't begin in a manger in Bethlehem. While it can be tempting to think that's where the story starts, it actually began long ago. Unfolding like a rich tapestry, gathering up nations and generations in its folds and carrying us all towards the event which would split history in two–this very event called Christmas that we celebrate each year in December.

While we might begin our celebration in Bethlehem, Luke reminds us in his gospel that this story actually began in a garden.

It might seem strange to begin a Christmas devotional here, but this is where I always need to start. I need the reminder that a history-altering moment in a garden so long ago is what made it necessary for Jesus to come–wrapped in human flesh to dwell among us. That moment in the garden of Eden so long ago, is what reveals the stakes and clearly shows us how much we need Jesus–at Christmas and always.

Fixating on Jesus's birth this time of year is so easy, but we miss something significant when we don't enter the full story that made his birth necessary to begin with. If we want the complete, glorious picture of Christ's birth we can't separate it from the rest of the story, the story that began with Adam and Eve, traces throughout the Old and New Testaments, and includes even us today.

Our verse for the day reminds us that one of the darkest days in human history, where sin and death broke perfect communion with God, cradled the promise that one day the greatest light the world has ever known, Jesus, would come. I don't know about you, but I enter this season with a much humbler and grateful heart when I remember Adam and Eve and a God who would formulate an extravagant rescue plan for me. And the doorway to enter this story is confession and repentance. Perhaps you could use this reminder today, too?

Pause & Reflect

Where do you need to repent and confess as you enter this Christmas season? Just like Adam and Eve, we have all sinned and need a Savior. Spend some time thanking God for rescuing you from sin and death!

THREE

Silence Speaks

"The Lord isn't really being slow about his promise, as some people think. No, he is being patient for your sake ..."

SECOND PETER 3:9

Between the event in the garden of Eden that ushered sin and brokenness into the world and the establishment of a new covenant of hope with the birth, death, and resurrection of Jesus, there was a gap. Honestly, that sentence seems like an understatement. Even to me. And I'm sure for the people who lived through it, it felt more like divine punishment than divine design.

As we trace the narrative arc of Scripture, we inevitably come to this long period of silence. Following the Old Testament era, for four hundred years the nation of Israel, recovering from exile and captivity, waited without a word from God. Waited for God to speak to them again, while clinging to the words he had spoken through prophets and priests. Words that promised a Messiah. A Rescuer.

Depending on the season of life you find yourself in, you might desperately long for a little silence, but most of us would probably agree that silence from God often feels personal and painful. And you might be wondering why I would include a couple of devotions about silence in a week dedicated to connection.

As I was preparing to write this book, I noticed something interesting; silence surrounds the story of Jesus. It bookends it, as if silence itself is a herald if we have ears to hear it. To drive the point home, the Bible shows us other seasons of silence too. And always, God was up to something. Silence sowed seeds of longing into desperate hearts, that God would then water, as only he could, with miraculous and thunderous outpourings of his mercy and kindness.

* Zechariah was struck silent, unable to speak, before the birth of his son, John–the voice of thunder in the desert (Luke 1). In Zechariah's silent season, his son was growing.

* Even more significantly, between Jesus's crucifixion and his resurrection, between Good Friday and Easter, there were three long days of silence. In this silence, God's magnificent plan of salvation was being sealed.

Perhaps silence is a significant part of our stories as well. Maybe this Christmas you find yourself in the midst of a silent season. Let me remind you today, friend, there is always purpose in God's ways. May you find comfort today in the fact that he never wastes a season–even silent ones.

Pause & Reflect

Spend five minutes in total silence. Let God speak to you about an area where he has seemed silent. Is there something that the silence is teaching you?

FOUR

Shattered Silence

"The people who walk in darkness will see a great light.
For those who live in a land of deep darkness, a light will shine."

ISAIAH 9:2

J esus's birth was the divine punctuation mark at the end of a four hundred-year-long silent season. And what a punctuation mark it was! Like a flash of lightning splitting the night in surprise, a star appeared. The soul-crushing burden of silence was shattered ... by Jesus!

"...The people thought that God had stopped speaking to them and acting on their behalf. They were living in what felt like the silence of God ... But silence is not proof of the absence of God; it's proof that God is working in ways we can't see or hear."[2]

The people of Israel had this prophecy from the lips of Isaiah (9:3-4, 6-7) to cling to in the midst of the silence and we have it still today.

"You will enlarge the nation of Israel,
    and its people will rejoice.
They will rejoice before you
    as people rejoice at the harvest
    and like warriors dividing the plunder.

For you will break the yoke of their slavery
and lift the heavy burden from their shoulders.
You will break the oppressor's rod,
just as you did when you destroyed
the army of Midian . . .
For a child is born to us,
a son is given to us.
The government will rest on his shoulders.
And he will be called:
Wonderful Counselor, Mighty God,
Everlasting Father, Prince of Peace.
His government and its peace
will never end.
He will rule with fairness and justice from the throne
of his ancestor David for all eternity.
The passionate commitment of the
Lord of Heaven's Armies
will make this happen!" (NLT)

I'm sure there were times when they felt extreme longing in the waiting, and they were filled with hope for the promise they believed would surely come to pass. But I'm sure there were other times where they felt every bit of hope and optimism leaking from them like air from a balloon.

Why don't we hear God speak anymore? Where did he go? Has he forgotten us?

Silence either conditions us, or it callouses us. In moments when God seems silent, will we look forward to his sure response in anticipation or will we give up and surrender to apathy? We get to choose.

If the tinkling of glasses, the melodies of carols, or the laughter of friends and family is loud this season, but God seems silent or distant, I want to remind you that silent seasons are often broken by dramatic and significant action from God. The birth of Jesus. His resurrection. These are just a few examples that our God shatters silence in grand fashion.

Pause & Reflect

How does thinking about the unfolding of God's story comfort you this Christmas season, especially if you're experiencing a season where God seems silent?

FIVE

Connecting over Consuming

"...Be satisfied with what you have."

HEBREWS 13:5

A genealogy. If I were writing a story, I probably wouldn't start with a list of names. How often have you sat down to read the Christmas story aloud and started with Matthew 1:1? Me neither. As we trace the story that God is writing in the Bible, we have four hundred years of silence and then ... a genealogy. Interesting to say the least. I don't know about you, but I don't typically get too excited about genealogies. (I get through certain parts of Numbers very quickly, if you know what I mean.)

So I find it curious that Matthew would choose to break the silence that loomed large over the Old Testament era with a list of names. He shows up to begin the New Testament, about to tell us the greatest story ever told, and he starts with ... a genealogy? Curious, indeed.

Besides the primary purpose of pointing out Jesus's lineage and proving that he is the long-awaited Messiah, I believe Matthew began the story like this because each of these people represent a life that was part of God's plan. They each had a part in this amazing story.

They all participated in unique and specific ways, and Matthew makes sure to point out the people that we would consider unlikely candidates to be included in Jesus's story. The genealogy reminds us that we all have a part to play in God's redemption story, and it matters how we play it.

Take a scroll through social media, turn on the television, or even listen to the radio, and it's brimming with messages about the latest gadget or must-have something-or-other that will change your life. Last time I opened Instagram, it seemed like an endless scroll of ads. In western culture, the Christmas season in particular has been designed to nurture and feed the consumer mindset, and it takes real work to recognize it and push back.

There's nothing wrong with gift giving. In fact, giving a gift at Christmas is full of beautiful symbolism. It can remind us that Jesus was the greatest gift we will ever receive, given to us by a perfect Father. But the true beauty of this season is unearthed in a call for less, for lightening. Do you feel it? The call to lay down all the "stuff" this season brings in exchange for something more meaningful? A releasing of things we've picked up throughout the year. The media shouts at our souls, "More is more!" But Jesus whispers, "I have another way."

Just like those listed in Matthew's genealogy, we can choose how we will participate in this story. We can choose, this Christmas, to enter into the calming presence of the One our hearts are truly longing for more of. We can choose our part in the story. We can be people who remain focused on the true reason we celebrate. In a culture caught up in consuming, we can choose a different path—we can choose connection with the One thing that truly endures and fulfills.

Pause & Reflect

What is one way that you can be more aware of the spirit of consumerism and fight against it this Christmas season?

SIX

Willingly Waiting

"Be still in the presence of the Lord, and wait patiently for him to act."

PSALM 37:7

It impresses me, therefore, that all the figures who appear in the first pages of Luke's Gospel are waiting. Zechariah and Elizabeth are waiting. Mary is waiting. Simeon and Anna, who were there at the temple when Jesus was brought in, are waiting. The whole opening scene of the good news is filled with waiting people."[3]

I don't like waiting, but I also don't like to be in a hurry. Riddle me that. But there's something about the Christmas season that can unwittingly suck us into a pattern of rushing and hurriedness, and before we know it we've missed everything the Lord wanted to do in our hearts during this miraculous season.

So, it seems there must be something holy about waiting, about patiently anticipating the actions of God. Waiting invites slowness into our life in a profound way, and connection with God on a deeper level. His timetable is clearly not the same as ours, and we'd be better calibrated to his rhythm if we just slowed down and took note of how he does things.

Here are just a few illustrations of God's timetable:

+ God could have sent Jesus five or ten years or even one
  hundred years after Adam and Eve sinned, or at any other
  point in history, but he waited.

+ Have you ever wondered why God sent Jesus in the slow-
  est manner possible? He was on earth for thirty-three years,
  and by our worldly standards he only did something that
  we would consider significant for three. That amounts to
  ninety percent of his life spent without any measurable
  achievements, and a very slow way to accomplish a very
  important mission.

+ Joshua was Moses's understudy for forty years. Forty. Years.

The examples could go on and on.

As Christians we join a heritage of believers who wait. Some for
a very long time, some not as long, and it's a reminder to us that
waiting is holy work. It allows us to better enter into God's presence
by respecting his timetable. Every detail of God's story will unfold
in exactly the right time and place to accomplish everything he has
planned. Let that thought settle into your heart as you connect with
God through waiting and slowness today.

Pause & Reflect

How can you step more readily into God's timetable this Christmas? Is there a way that you can choose to appreciate slowness and waiting more?

SEVEN

Connection over Conflict

"Don't be selfish; don't try to impress others. Be humble, thinking of others as better than yourselves. Don't look out only for your own interests, but take an interest in others, too. You must have the same attitude that Christ Jesus had."

PHILIPPIANS 2:3-5

In Iowa, where I live, the final days of deer season just happen to coincide with Christmas. Genius. One particular year I had plans to binge watch Christmas movies, drink hot cocoa, and eat yummy food with my people. Unfortunately, half of them had completely different plans that involved camouflage, a bow, and the woods.

Let's be real. Sometimes our best laid plans get ruined. When it comes to family, the holiday season can often be filled with more conflict than connecting (especially when deer are involved–or maybe that's just my family). But Jesus came so that we could have a relationship with him, *and* a better relationship with those around us.

This week our main focus has been on connecting with God, but we can't overlook connecting with people as well. Because that was what Jesus was all about–and the holidays aren't complete without it.

Perhaps just a few short days into the Christmas season you've already been let down by someone's bah-humbug attitude, or maybe you've clashed over something more significant and your season is not starting off at all how you would like.

Or maybe Christmas reminds you of a relationship that's been broken or has grown distant and you'd like to work towards repairing it.

Whenever we're dealing with people, there's the potential for disappointment, hurt feelings, and unmet expectations, (Wow, this is really uplifting, right?) but there's also the potential for incredible love, joy, and celebration. Once again, going back to Day Five, we get to choose how we will participate. We'll never be able to control someone else's attitudes, words, or feelings, but we can submit ours to God and pray that he will help us connect with people this Christmas season in a way that honors him and leaves us feeling fulfilled in the best possible way.

On that day several Christmases ago, when my plans were interrupted by deer, I did not put this advice into practice, and my soul and my family paid the price. As a woman entering a new phase of life where my children have both graduated from high school and will soon leave and start lives of their own, I know eventually I won't even really have this choice to make; so I choose to make it now. Wouldn't you rather be a source of joy instead of pain? Wouldn't you rather treasure the time you get instead of complaining about the time you didn't? You can choose connection over conflict and strife today. Your family and your soul will thank you!

Pause & Reflect

Is there something you can do to connect more fully with your family and/or friends this season? Is there someone you need to reconnect or reconcile with this Christmas season?

Week Two

WONDER

EIGHT

Wonder over Weariness

*"Everyone was gripped with great wonder and awe, and they praised
God, exclaiming, 'We have seen amazing things today!'"*

LUKE 5:26

Doesn't it seem like childlike wonder and delight are becoming increasingly scarce these days? Sometimes it feels like everything around us is designed to rob or replace our sense of curiosity and wonder with facts and figures. Not that there's anything wrong with science or facts and figures (sometimes they can inspire wonder too), but some of the best things in life are completely unexplainable and mystery is the very thing that makes them great.

In today's world of modern advancements and ever-increasing scientific discoveries, it's easy for our sense of wonder and awe to be replaced with weariness and apathy. I'm convinced that our collective loss of wonder has led to a deep weariness in our souls, and Christmas is God's remedy.

Over this next week we're going to look at several people in the Christmas story who knew how to live well with their sense of wonder and awe intact. Let's commit to entering their stories with a sense of reverence and awe.

Angels appearing and splitting the night sky with a choir of good news, a virgin giving birth, a bright new star. If we're not careful, the Christmas story itself can become common and we can grow numb to its miraculous power.

The incredible thing about the Bible and about our God, is that there's always more treasure to be uncovered. There's never a point, no matter how much we study or learn, where we've discovered it all. As I was writing this devotional I learned so many things that made me sit back in awe at God's attention to detail.

For instance, did you know...

* The name of the town where Jesus was born—Bethlehem—literally means "house of bread." "[It] is a prophetic declaration of future provision ... The house of bread was where the Bread of Life was born."[4]

* "According to the first century historian Josephus, the Passover lamb was slaughtered around 3 p.m. This was the time of day when Christ died on the cross."[5]

You'll see even more examples of God's attention to detail as we move through this week together.

As we begin, ask yourself: Have I immunized myself from the wonder? Have I safely cocooned myself away from the disruptive and awe-inspiring nature of the gospel? Have I treated the Bible and the stories it contains casually? Have I become numb to the miraculous power and awe-inspiring wonder of the Christmas story? If so, begin to prepare your heart for this week by confessing that to the Lord and asking him to stir your soul with renewed wonder.

Pause & Reflect

What's one thing that you can do that would cause your mouth to hang open in wonder? Maybe going on a drive to see Christmas lights, or attending a play or ballet? Make plans to do that thing today.

NINE

They Followed a Star

"...About that time some wise men from eastern lands arrived
in Jerusalem, asking, 'Where is the newborn king of the Jews?
We saw his star as it rose, and we have come to worship him.'"

MATTHEW 2:1-2

Imagine that you spend your days gazing at the night sky, searching for guidance and wisdom among the constellations you see there and, to your delight, you discover something new. You grab a couple friends and the three of you stare in wonder, up into the heavens.

Imagine the shock and joy you'd feel at discovering a bright and brand new star and knowing it was beckoning you somewhere. A celestial herald announcing that something has happened that will change absolutely everything.

This is exactly what happened to the magi. They spent their days with their eyes on the sky, looking for cosmic changes, and Matthew 2:10 tells us, "When they saw the star, they were filled with joy!" I believe the Bible labeled these men wise because they still felt joy in the everyday moments and discoveries of their lives.

They could have easily missed Jesus if they had allowed themselves to grow weary, apathetic, or distracted. But they remained focused with their eyes to the sky.

The star that signaled Jesus's birth interrupted the course of their everyday life and demanded they make a choice. Would they follow where it led? Or would they think, *Well, that's interesting, but I'm not going to let it disrupt my life,* and then continue on about their lives and forget all about it? Not these men. They chose to follow the star and something incredible happened: they encountered Jesus. These wise men are permanently etched in history because of a decision to pause their lives and follow.

And when they found Jesus, the One they had been pursuing through signs and wonders, the Bible says, "They entered the house and saw the child with his mother, Mary, and they bowed down and worshiped him. Then they opened their treasure chests and gave him gifts of gold, frankincense, and myrrh." (Matt. 2:11) Once they encountered him, they were compelled to offer him something of value.

During this Christmas season, we can carry three things with us from the magi:

1. We can keep our eyes open, ever searching, for the incredible displays of God's power.

2. We can pause and follow him when he disrupts our lives.

3. We can offer him the most valuable thing, the one thing he desires above everything else: our whole hearts.

The events unfolding in your life might not be as dramatic as a new star lighting up the night sky–but are you too busy in this season to recognize the invitation of God to come and worship and encounter Jesus? Where is he signaling to you in this season? Is he inviting you to map the constellations of your faith? What can we learn today from the wonder and excitement of the magi as they followed the breadcrumbs scattered across the night sky? What can you offer to the Lord today?

Pause & Reflect

Even, and maybe especially, if it's cold outside where you live, take a moment to go outside. Perhaps even drive outside of town, turn down the light pollution and noise around you and gaze in wonder at the (mostly) same night sky those magi studied thousands of years ago. May the tiny pinpricks of light flecking the sky like salt give you an ever-increasing sense of peace and wonder.

TEN

A Heavenly Host

"Suddenly, an angel of the Lord appeared among them,
and the radiance of the Lord's glory surrounded them."

LUKE 2:9

If you've ever questioned if God is working in the details of your life, or in the wider world, then the shepherds' story will speak to you from the pages of Scripture today. Their story is proof that not only is God at work in specific and significant ways, but he often chooses to reveal himself to the most unlikely people, in the most unlikely ways.

As I mentioned at the beginning of this week, one of the things that gets me the most excited and awakens the most wonder in me is to see the tiny details, the intricate layers, that God lays down in the stories he writes. Maybe it's the writer in me, but I really nerd out over all of it. And the story of the shepherds is a perfect example.

In her Advent study, author Kayla Ferris points out, "God sent his entire heavenly host to sing about [Jesus's arrival] in a field full of shepherds who were ... get this ... caring for lambs awaiting a Passover slaughter. Even in his birth announcement, God points us to his plan."[6]

I don't know about you, but that wows me in a way I can't quite describe in words.

To the culturally insignificant shepherds, who knew the value of a lamb, God sent angels to announce his Son's birth. And then Matthew 2:17 tells us what happened next: "After seeing him, the shepherds told everyone what had happened and what the angel had said to them about this child. All who heard the shepherds' story were astonished."

Unlikely ways and unlikely people, indeed. If I had big news to announce, I probably wouldn't have chosen a bunch of shepherds as the ones to spread it. I would have likely gone straight to the influencers of the day, but God doesn't work like we do. Nowhere is it more clear than in the unlikely way in which Jesus came into the world, that God doesn't place value in the same places that we do. And aren't you so grateful? He still uses the most unlikely people in the most unlikely ways to spread his incredible message! That's good news today.

Pause & Reflect

How does the story of God choosing to announce the birth of Jesus to the shepherds encourage you today?

ELEVEN

A Virgin Conceives

"When Joseph woke up, he did as the angel of the Lord commanded..."

MATTHEW 1:24

A Virgin conceives. This is inconceivable by human calculation and understanding, and yet it's the very foundation of this story that we are so focused on this time of year. Every bit of it smacks with miracle and impossibility. The very thing that makes it incredible is also the thing that we can grow accustomed and indifferent towards. Glossing over the words, taking them for granted, we can lose the sheer ridiculousness that would have struck the very people we're reading about.

Have you ever wondered how this incredible story of the arrival of the Son of God in the world would have gone if Mary had said, "Uh, thanks, but no thanks. I think I'm good. Giving birth to the Son of God doesn't really fit into my life plan right now." What if she had said no, instead of agreeing to this plan that seemed crazy and, honestly, possibly dangerous? I'm a details girl. As in, give me all the details before I'm going to do what you suggest. But not Mary.

Because of her willingness to press ahead without all of the details, Mary ushered in a miracle through faith, trust, and surrender. Not words we often associate with Christmas–but they should be. I think the Lord already knew that she would say yes. That's why she was given the incredible opportunity to be the mother of God. When the Lord looks at me I want him to see the same willing heart. I'm guessing you probably do too.

If you take a few moments to read her story, you'll see she quickly moved from, "How?" to, "Yes, I see it now. I'm the Lord's maid, ready to serve. Let it be with me just as you say" (Luke 1:29-38).

There were so many things that she could have asked, fretted, or stressed about. Not the least of which, the fact she could have been killed or completely ostracized and abandoned by her community. Instead, she simply said yes to the Lord.

We too can get so bogged down in the how that we forget to say, "Yes, let it be just as you say." Demanding to know details, we forfeit the miracle that God wants to birth in and through us. Mary's life reminds us that God doesn't need us to focus on the details. All he needs is a heart surrendered in trust and obedience. As we saw yesterday, he's got all of the details covered spectacularly.

Mary wasn't the only willing and obedient soul in this story, though. We're told repeatedly throughout chapter two of Matthew that Joseph obeyed. When it comes to birth stories, fathers usually take a back seat. The entire narrative is generally all about mama and the baby, and dad is just there somewhere in the background. Honestly, Joseph takes up very little space in the gospel accounts, yet what is said about him is so significant. We don't hear much else (if anything) about Joseph after Jesus's birth, but his obedience was noteworthy. When God spoke he listened and obeyed.

Willing and obedient hearts were the exact qualities that God was looking for to bring a miracle to the world. May he cultivate the same in us today.

Pause & Reflect

Is there an area of your life where you are struggling to be obedient to the Lord? How does Mary and Joseph's story encourage you today?

TWELVE

Everyday Obedience

*"One day Zechariah was serving God in the Temple,
for his order was on duty that week."*

LUKE 1:8

Have you ever asked someone to explain something to you and they start talking about something that seems totally unrelated? And you're secretly thinking, *Would you just get to the point already?!*

Luke's gospel is a little bit like this. We come to the book expecting to hear about Jesus, but he starts with a seemingly unrelated story about an old, barren couple. Within the story of Zechariah and Elizabeth there are echoes and parallels to the story of Jesus. With Zechariah and Elizabeth, God was changing the story of an individual family and then with Jesus, he changed the story for all humanity.

Admittedly, there's so much beauty in this couple's story, but I believe one of the reasons Luke started his gospel here was because Zechariah was just going about his business, doing what he was supposed to be doing, and God showed up. In the midst of his faithfulness and humble service, God sent an angel to tell him that his whole life was about to change.

You might be curious why I chose to put this story in the week about wonder, but isn't it a true wonder when God breaks into our ordinary lives and does something extraordinary? And we never know when he might do it. It creates a sense of expectation in our hearts; any mundane moment of our lives could be history-shaking with God.

The birth of John, a son given to a previously barren couple, was only the setup. The preparation. People in Zechariah and Elizabeth's community were amazed and couldn't stop talking about it, and I think God was thinking, "If you think this is good ... just wait til you see what comes next." Because in the very next chapter we see Jesus burst onto the scene. How wondrous of God to show up in such an incredible way in the lives of ordinary people, going about their ordinary work.

Pause & Reflect

How does the idea that God showed up in the midst of Zechariah's everyday obedience stir a sense of expectation and wonder in you today?

THIRTEEN

An Expectant Heart

*"In Jerusalem at the time, there was a man, Simeon by name, a good
man, a man who lived in the prayerful expectancy of help for Israel."*

LUKE 2:25

Can I ask a question, now that we're neck deep in the throes of
the holiday season? What are you living in?

Today's passage tells us about a man who was *living in prayerful
expectancy* for God's power to be on display around him. Simeon's
attitude of expectancy caused him to be filled with the Spirit and an
incredible promise that he would see the Messiah, the salvation of
Israel, with his own eyes.

Again, I ask. What are you living in? I'm not talking about your
physical surroundings. Instead, I'm talking about the attitude of your
heart. Are you living in hurried chaos? An overscheduled season? Or
have you allowed your heart to be filled with prayerful expectancy?
Open to any and every way in which God might show up and move?

I love this quote by Loretta Ross-Gotta:

"Jesus observed, 'Without me you can do nothing' (John 15:5).
Yet we act, for the most part, as though without us God can do nothing. We think we have to make Christmas come, which is to say we

think we have to bring about the redemption of the universe on our own. When all God needs is a willing womb, a place of safety, nourishment, and love. 'Oh, but nothing will get done,' you say. 'If I don't do it, Christmas won't happen.' And we crowd out Christ with our fretful fears...What if, instead of *doing* something, we were to *be* something special? Be a womb. Be a dwelling for God."[7]

All this hurry and bustle, when all we really need to be is available for the Spirit of God to dwell within us. This is the true spirit of Christmas that transforms and enlivens us with joy and wonder. We're almost halfway through the season, a perfect time to pause and ask yourself, before the season passes you by, *Am I making my heart a dwelling place for God? Or have I gotten so focused on other things that he's become an afterthought?*

Pause & Reflect

Spend a few moments thinking about how you can make your heart a place for God to dwell more richly, both in this season and all the seasons to come. Choose one practical thing to implement in your life today.

FOURTEEN

An Unlikely Example

*"The king's heart is like a stream of water directed by
the Lord; he guides it wherever he pleases."*

PROVERBS 21:1

eadlines shout at us with dire and grim predictions: The polar
ice caps are melting, a new type of bacteria is going to wipe
out half the earth's population. If we could travel back in time, and
there were newspapers in Jesus's day, the headlines might have been
dominated by panic at the palace. After the wise men came to inquire
about the newborn king of the Jews, Matthew tells us Herod (and
the entire city) was in an uproar. Matthew 2:3 says, "When Herod
the king heard this, he was troubled, and all Jerusalem with him."

In our era, we celebrate the birth of Jesus, but his birth threw
some into a panic. Was it because a new king would disrupt their
carefully crafted balance of power? Perhaps they were too comfort-
able with the status quo, or the status they held. We can't know for
sure, but we do know Herod was afraid of a small child. And he was
right to feel that way, but not for the reasons he expected, because
Jesus would demand something from everyone he encountered: a
choice, a determination.

Due to the perceived threat to his power, Herod hatched a plan for total annihilation of all the Jewish boys under two years old (Matt. 2:16). This guy was completely cuckoo. For this reason, you don't ordinarily hear a lot about Caesar or Herod in Christmas devotionals. Herod was a crazed, maniacal ruler who murdered innocent children—talk about a villain in a story. But have you ever considered why God chose to send Jesus during his reign?

God could have chosen a more stable time in history, a more stable ruler, but he didn't. Why did God choose that moment in history to send his Son? Why did he choose the reign of a man that would murder innocent children to protect his power as the time to reveal his salvation plan? And why would I include this within the pages of this book?

Our world can often seem chaotic and out of balance, and rulers and leaders ungodly, or even cruel or vindictive. Yet this was exactly the type of stage where God chose to put one of his most magnificent plans into motion. Everything lined up to fulfill God's ultimate plan, in spite, and sometimes because of, Herod. I believe God chose this time in history to prove his preeminence over earthly authority—to show us, even all these years later, that he is above and before it all.

Pause & Reflect

Do current events have you feeling stressed or hopeless? How does today's look at Herod help you put that in proper perspective?

Week Three

TRANSFORMATION

FIFTEEN

Transformation over Traditions

"Don't copy the behavior and customs of this world, but let God transform you into a new person by changing the way you think. Then you will learn to know God's will for you, which is good and pleasing and perfect."

ROMANS 12:2

A couple of years ago a friend of mine got sucked into some drama on Facebook, and she wanted to know my thoughts on the matter. One very opinionated Facebook user insisted that Christmas trees were a pagan symbol that needed to be replaced with a manger, and a "debate" ensued. Understandably, things got heated, as things tend to do online, and the exchange started to spiral, and now my friend was left examining her own traditions.

I'm not here to enter the Christmas tree versus manger debate. Everyone needs to work out their traditions before the Lord, because some of our traditions, even those deeply rooted in Christian practice and faith, can become routine and rote, losing their meaning and impact over time. Even the purest traditions can become tarnished by thoughtless repetition. But I loved that Facebook conversation because it stirred some thoughtful reflection and conversation between my friend and me. Together, we started to examine our traditions and talk about the ways they do or don't help us remember what the season is truly about.

As followers of Jesus, we're called, as the verse in Romans points out, not to "copy the behavior and customs of this world," but instead to live in light of what Christ has done. And I especially love the idea that we can be more thoughtful about the traditions and customs we embrace at Christmas—and that's exactly what this week is all about.

I'll be honest, I didn't know the meaning or history behind many of the traditions we'll talk about this week. I just participated in them without much thought, but learning about them has made their practice all the sweeter and caused me to think about Jesus even more.

I don't ever want to settle for mechanical actions over heart transformation, and I never want to forget the why behind the what. I'm not suggesting you get rid of any of your current traditions. Instead, I'm offering a simple idea that there might be a way to be more thoughtful about them. My hope is that as you journey through this week, some of the Christmas traditions that you've participated in over the years become imbued with new and deeper meaning and help you dwell more deeply in Christ this Christmas season.

Pause & Reflect

What is your most beloved Christmas tradition and how does it help you honor or remember Christ? If it doesn't, is there a way that it could?

SIXTEEN

Wreaths

"... From everlasting to everlasting you are God."

PSALM 90:2

Christmas has become disposable. We toss out our used wrapping paper, our trees, and if you have a large family you might even use disposable plates and napkins for the Christmas meal. While there's nothing wrong with gift wrap or paper plates, this throwaway mentality is why I love the origins of the Christmas wreath.

Historically, Europeans pruned their Christmas trees and then, "instead of throwing the pieces of greenery away [they] wove the excess into wreaths."[8] The tradition of the Christmas wreath was born out of a desire to create beauty and usefulness from scraps that could have been seen as dispensable and disposable.

I'm going to be vulnerable and confess that I don't always approach this season with that mindset. Even the gifts I bought my kids when they were little were often destined for a quick trip to the garbage bin. Gift-giving was all about volume over quality or intentionality. More presents equaled a better Christmas, as the mountain of gift wrap piled up around the tree. Nevermind that many of the presents were destined to be ignored or trashed by the time the day was over. The humble Christmas wreath stands as a reminder for us to be more intentional about the way we celebrate, to be creative and use what we have to create beauty and purpose.

And there's another beautiful reminder tucked into the boughs of the Christmas wreath. "The shape was also significant as a representation of divine perfection. It symbolized eternity, as the shape has no end ... Together, the circular shape and the evergreen material make the wreath a representation of eternal life."[8]

Today's verse and the simple Christmas wreath can be a gentle reminder for us each time we see it of the eternal life we have in Christ and also the everlasting and eternal nature of God. Just as the circle of the wreath has no beginning or end, so too, our God has no beginning or end. He always was and always will be.

Pause & Reflect

What do you find most significant about the origins of the Christmas wreath? How will seeing one change the way you celebrate or think?

SEVENTEEN

Nativity Sets

*"And these words that I command you today shall be on your
heart. You shall teach them diligently to your children, and shall
talk of them when you sit in your house, and when you walk
by the way, and when you lie down, and when you rise."*

DEUTERONOMY 6:6-7

Over the years, our family has owned several nativity sets, but
I think the most beloved one was made from wooden blocks
and looked like little cartoon characters. The kids loved it because
they could touch it and rearrange the pieces without fear of break-
ing something. Sometimes Jesus ended up on the roof of the stable.
Things could get pretty wild.

But I always loved to see them arranging those little blocks, because
it was an obvious invitation to talk about the Lord and the true reason we celebrate Christmas.

Tradition tells us that we can thank Saint Francis of Assisi for
the idea of the live nativity. It was his creation and dates all the way
back to 1223. Gradually, over time, people moved away from live-
stock and live people at churches to statues they could have in their
homes.[9] I imagine it was far less of a mess on the carpet.

It's supposed that Saint Francis came up with the concept of the nativity in reaction to an increasingly materialistic society. Sound familiar? He wanted to draw people's focus once again to Christ.[10] Thus the nativity was born.

We know that Saint Francis created the nativity scene to keep our eyes and hearts focused on Christ during the Christmas season, but if we're not careful it can become just another piece of Christmas decor that our eyes glance over and don't truly see.

That's why I've come to appreciate the nativity set as an invitation to intentionality. As the most overtly religious part of my Christmas decorations, it can sometimes be the easiest to set up and then ignore. However, I want it to drive me to experience the true wonder of the season each time I look at it. Causing me, as Saint Francis would have wanted, to turn my thoughts and my heart towards Christ.

Pause & Reflect

If you have a nativity set in your home, when was the last time you spent any time gazing in wonder at the pieces and the incredible story it represents?

Christmas Trees

"Hear, O Israel: The Lord our God, the Lord is one."

DEUTERONOMY 6:4

As a midwesterner, I'm accustomed to having four seasons. As an Iowan, I'm conditioned for exceptionally long winter seasons. Starting in late October, the grass turns a strange yellowish brown hue and the trees become naked versions of their former selves. Everything goes dormant, and we don't typically see green again until May. The exception to all of this is the evergreen tree.

These beauties buoy us through the long winter months with the only dose of green our eyes will behold until spring arrives. Thus they became the tree of choice for northern and eastern Europeans–and specifically Germans, who are said to have started the tradition that we know as the Christmas tree.[8]

In an article about the origins of the Christmas Tree, *Time* magazine tells us it was common practice for people to trim the trees before bringing them into their homes. "Besides the aesthetic and practical reasons for shaping the tree, there was also a spiritual significance to the practice for Christians .... It was important to trim the trees into the shape of a triangle, to represent the Trinity ... Catholic legend says that Saint Boniface, a monk from England, used the three points of an evergreen tree to explain the concept of God the Father, Son, and Holy Ghost back in the seventh century."[8]

Of additional significance, since evergreens are able to survive even the harshest conditions, they came to represent hope even amid bleak surroundings.[8] As my husband likes to say (because he is a preacher), "That'll preach!" Who knew Christmas trees were so fraught with spiritual significance? (Maybe I'll join that Christmas tree versus manger debate after all! Just kidding!) Knowing this brief history has definitely helped me attach greater significance to this beloved tradition, and brings my thoughts back to Jesus during this season.

The Trinity can be a tricky concept to understand, but viewing our trees as a living, visual example of the relationship between Father, Son, and Holy Spirit can be a great catalyst for conversation and contemplation. Their heartiness in the face of difficult conditions can encourage us and renew our hope, causing us to appreciate the humble Christmas tree in a deeper way if we too are facing tough times. I love what Dietrich Bonhoeffer said, "Therefore we adults can rejoice deeply within our hearts under the Christmas tree, perhaps much more than the children are able. We know that God's goodness will once again draw near. We think of all of God's goodness that came our way last year and sense something of this marvelous [feeling of] home."[11]

Pause & Reflect

Which aspect of the Christmas tree strikes you most today: its representation of the Trinity or its resilience and hardiness in the face of adversity? Why?

NINETEEN

Advent Calendars

"So teach us to number our days that we may get a heart of wisdom."

PSALM 90:12

Each December I anxiously counted down the days until I could exuberantly shout, "See you next year!" as I exited the school doors for Christmas break.

You've probably counted down the days to an event or special occasion in your life too. Maybe you've counted down the days until a much needed vacation. Kids count down the days until summer break, and many of us have used today's topic of discussion, advent calendars, to count down the days until Christmas.

Growing up, my mom used to buy me a new advent calendar each year. Every morning I woke with the thrill of opening a new door and discovering a tiny surprise nestled behind the door. But I'll be honest, I had no idea that the practice was named after a spiritually significant season in the church calendar. I just thought it was a weird name for a super fun and treasured tradition. (I grew up Pentecostal in case you're extremely confused by my ignorance.)

Once again, we can thank the Germans for this beloved tradition, which started with various practices like, "ticking off chalk marks on walls or doors, lighting candles and placing straws in a nativity crib."[12] All of that led to some families putting up "a devotional image" every day, thus the custom of Advent calendars were born in the mid-1800s, and it's said they were brought to America by soldiers returning from World War II.[12]

Now that I've gotten older, and I know what that weird name for one of my most favorite traditions was all about, and I understand the meaning of Advent in a way that I didn't grasp as a child, I long to experience its purpose in a deeper way.

Today's verse is a reminder that wisdom comes from being aware that our lives are fleeting and so are the seasons within it. We all know the Christmas season feels more fleeting than most. As you open the doors of your Advent calendar this Christmas, may you be reminded of the beauty of this brief season and ask the Lord to fill you with wisdom as you number your days.

Pause & Reflect

How can staying mindful of how quickly the Christmas season (and our lives) passes help you celebrate in a more meaningful way?

TWENTY

Christmas Lights

*"Jesus spoke to the people once more and said, 'I am the light
of the world. If you follow me, you won't have to walk in
darkness, because you will have the light that leads to life."*

JOHN 8:12

I'm pretty sure every community has a Griswald family style light
display. A house that has so many Christmas lights it's a city-wide
spectacle to behold. The light coming from their yard is akin to day-
light and you might need shades just to drive by. Pity the neighbors,
but for the rest of us it's an extravaganza of joy.

Christmas lights as we know them are a fairly new invention, due
in part to the invention of the lightbulb. However, the original instinct
and desire to bring light to the dark and long winter months started
with people putting candles on Christmas tree branches. However,
Christmas trees and open flames really aren't a good match. So the
right-hand man of Thomas Edison, Edward H. Johnson, created
the first string of red, white and blue lights and placed them on the
Christmas tree in his parlor window and the rest is history.[13]

Stringing up lights at Christmas is our small attempt at vanquish-
ing the darkness, but any light we hang or observe this Christmas

pales in comparison to the light our Savior brings to the world. Of all the traditions we've talked about so far this week, Christmas lights have the most commercial origins, but it's relatively easy to connect them with a greater awareness of Jesus. Their light can remind us that Jesus called himself the light of the world. In this way, our Christmas lights really can cause us to enjoy the season even more as we rest in the light of salvation that was brought to us so long ago by a God who loved us enough to send us his Son.

Even though this tradition began as a gimmick, we can use the ubiquitous lights as glowing signs pointing us to our Savior—the true light of the world.

Pause & Reflect

How does remembering Jesus as the light of the world help you appreciate Christmas lights in a deeper way?

TWENTY-ONE

Christmas Caroling

"I will sing of the Lord's unfailing love forever!
Young and old will hear of your faithfulness."

PSALM 89:1

"Here we come a-wassailing among the leaves so green ... " What exactly is a-wassailing, anyway? This particular Christmas carol has always been a little perplexing to me, but it seems to be the quintessential caroling tune. Maybe you've been a participant in the Christmas caroling tradition (we won't talk about whether it was willing participation or not), or been the recipient of a gaggle of people singing on your doorstep.

Of all the traditions we've talked about, I think this is one of the most unique. Who actually dreamt up the idea of going door to door in the freezing cold and singing to friends, neighbors, and strangers?

Interestingly, it dates back to the thirteenth century and originally had little to do with Christmas or singing at all. "In its earliest days, wassailing involved people going house to house giving out well wishes during the colder months. In some places, 'wassail' was also commonly used to describe a hot and thick spiced beverage given to travelers during the winter to help keep them warm ... Singing remained separate from Christmas until Saint Francis of Assisi began incorporating similar sayings and songs of well wishes in his Christmas services. He encouraged the members of his church to embrace music during the holiday season."[14]

And embrace it we have. The power of caroling comes through its ability to get us out of our homes and into community. During the winter, I tend to think bears have the right idea. I'm more than happy to curl up with a good book and a warm blanket and hibernate through the long winter months. Caroling is a lighthearted effort to get us out of our lairs and out spreading Christmas joy and love to others, and honestly, while we're at it, ourselves.

While it might sound unappealing to step out into the blustery cold, it really is fun! It's one of those traditions that brings joy to you *and* others! It might be the very thing you need this Christmas season.

Pause & Reflect

Try getting a group of people together to go caroling and spread a little Christmas cheer to someone who might really need it.

Week Four

PREPARE & RECEIVE

TWENTY-TWO

Who Do You Say I Am?

"Then he [Jesus] asked them, 'But who do you say I am?'"

MATTHEW 16:15

A s we head into Christmas week, there's a question that rings in my head. One that Jesus posed to his disciples so many thousands of years ago. At the height of his ministry when people were flocking around him, he asked them if they recognized him, if they understood who he truly was?

I like to think of this moment between Jesus and the disciples like an *Undercover Boss* reveal moment. If you haven't seen the show, company owners disguise themselves as everyday workers so they can go in undetected and get a behind-the-scenes look at what's happening in their businesses. Towards the end of the show they take off the disguise and reveal it was them the entire time.

Jesus had a couple of these moments with people, and we see one of them in Luke 4:18. He's at the synagogue reading from Isaiah 61, words penned hundreds of years earlier, prophesying about him, and it was as if he was standing up and saying, "Hey, it's me! No disguises. Do you recognize me? Who am I to you?"

And even in that moment so many people missed it. They didn't recognize him. Or they couldn't.

Martin Luther was quick to point out that the message of the angels to the shepherds was quite personal. "... I bring *you* good news ..." (Luke 2:10 emphasis added). He goes on to say, "Therefore see to it that you do not treat the Gospel only as history, for that is only transient; neither regard it only as an example, for it is of no value without faith. Rather, see to it that you make this birth your own and that Christ be born in you."[15]

With the final days before Christmas ahead of us, we must ask ourselves this question: Who do you say he is? Is he just a baby in a manger that, outside of a few days in December, doesn't really impact your day-to-day life? Or is he the Lord and King of your life, the Boss, if you will?

Pause & Reflect

Take a moment to answer the question that Jesus asks us yet today: "Who do you say that I am?"

TWENTY-THREE

Expect to be Surprised

*"'My thoughts are nothing like your thoughts,' says the Lord.
'And my ways are far beyond anything you could imagine.'"*

ISAIAH 55:8

Who can know and understand the mind of God? With that
said, I think the entire Christmas story is a fascinating glimpse
into the mind of God. The longer I serve the Lord, and the more I
study the Bible, the more clearly I see that God's ways are uncon-
ventional. He defies all of my preconceived ideas about how things
should be done and surprises me in the most unexpected of ways.

Before Jesus arrived on the scene, the Jewish people were awaiting the Messiah. Undoubtedly, they had ideas about what he would
look like, what he would do, and how he would do it. I'd venture
to say not a single one of them said, "Hey, I bet he'll come as a baby,
spend thirty years growing up in relative obscurity, and then minis-
ter for three short years. And following that, he'll die on a cross and
be raised from the dead! That's exactly how I would save the world."

I'm confident not one person thought that.

In fact, it's pretty clear from biblical accounts that not only did
they *not* think that, when it was revealed to them that that's exactly

what happened they couldn't accept it. They labeled him a blasphemer and crucified him. God's plan was so far beyond anyone's ability to dream up, let alone pull off.

God's plan
* started small
* started with helplessness
* started with slow growth
* started with subtle promise

One of my favorite writers and thinkers, Brennan Manning, put it this way: "The Bethlehem mystery will ever be a scandal to aspiring disciples who seek a triumphant Savior and a prosperity Gospel."[1]

Mark 6:5 tells us a curious thing: people in Jesus's own hometown were incredulous and couldn't get over the fact that they'd known him since he was a kid. Surely he wasn't the Son of God. He was just Mary and Joseph's boy.

They were so surprised by the way that God chose to enter the world, the mystery and utter powerlessness of it all, that many of them couldn't accept or recognize what God was doing. It didn't look the way they wanted it to at all. But I think we can all agree God's way was infinitely better than a temporary military conquest or localized government. But just like those in Jesus's day, we can remain fixated on our own ways and solutions. We'd never say we think our plans are better than God's out loud, but inwardly we think it.

How often do we succumb to the same temptation as the Jews from Jesus's day, to want God to do things our way? As this settles into your heart today, ponder what Henri Nouwen said, "Hope is trusting that something will be fulfilled, but fulfilled according to the promises and not just according to our wishes."[3] A difficult, yet worthy, prayer to offer today.

Pause & Reflect

How does contemplating God's ways encourage you today? If you're struggling to trust him in an area of your life, what would it look like to submit your ideas and will to him in surrender?

TWENTY-FOUR

Prepare Him Room

"And while they were there, the time came for her baby to be born. She gave birth to her firstborn son. She wrapped him snugly in strips of cloth and laid him in a manger, because there was no lodging available for them."

LUKE 2:6-7

Jesus arrived in a world that had no room for him, both literally and figuratively. There was no room in the inn and, according to Herod, no room for another king. And yet, "Christ is always with us, always asking for room in our hearts."[16]

At this time of year we can spend more time preparing holiday menus, planning parties, and creating gift lists than we spend preparing our hearts to receive the incredible gift of Jesus. As I thought about this, I came to the conclusion that we choose these tasks because they're easier. It's far simpler to plan a perfect party than it is to receive the true gift of Christmas fully into our lives.

Recently, I was reading something that captured this idea perfectly and convicted me deeply. William Willimon wrote, "Charles Dickens' story of Scrooge's transformation has probably done more to form our notions of Christmas than St. Luke's story of the manger ... *A Christmas Carol* is more congenial to our favorite images of ourselves. Dickens suggests that deep down, even the worst of us can become generous, giving people. Yet I suggest we are better givers than getters, not because we are generous people but because we are proud, arrogant people. The Christmas story–the one according to Luke not Dickens–is not about how blessed it is to be givers but about how essential it is to see ourselves as receivers."[17]

Indeed, isn't this the entire message of the gospel–the truly good news? That while we were still sinners Christ came and died for us (Romans 5:8). We didn't do anything to deserve it, and all we have to do is humble ourselves and receive it. But that idea of humbling ourselves, of admitting our need, scrapes against our sense of pride, and makes us squirmy, uncomfortable receivers.

Accepting the gift of Christ is simple, and yet it isn't easy. We have to joyfully embrace our role as recipients of God's incredible mercy and grace. Without that heart posture, the deep and abiding miracle of Christmas will just pass us by.

Tomorrow we celebrate the birth of our Savior, but today we prepare him room. May our hearts be wide open, declaring there is room for him, and where there is no room, we will make it, humbling ourselves as grateful recipients of his magnificent love and grace.

Pause & Reflect

What is one specific thing you can do today that will prepare room for Christ in your heart and make you more aware of his presence?

TWENTY-FIVE

A Savior, Who is Christ the Lord

"The Savior—yes, the Messiah, the Lord—has been
born today in Bethlehem, the city of David!"

LUKE 2:11

In the midst of chaos and bustling streets, a cry split the air and, with it, time as we know it. From that moment forward everything is referred to as before Christ and after Christ. On this day we celebrate the birth of reconciliation with God, restoration, and rescue from sin and death.

Here is but a small sample of what we celebrate:

* Reconciliation – According to Merriam-Webster, reconciliation is a restoring to friendship of a relationship that was broken or damaged. Colossians 1:21-22 tells us, "You were [God's] enemies, separated from him by your evil thoughts and actions. Yet now he has reconciled you to himself through the death of Christ in his physical body. As a result, he has brought you into his own presence, and you are holy and blameless as you stand before him without a single fault."

* Restoration – When I think of restoration I think of Joanna Gaines and *Fixer Upper*, making something that was once dirty and unloved into an inviting haven of beauty and rest. And I think this is such a beautiful picture of what Christ does. He takes out the junk and the trash and makes us a dwelling place for his own presence to dwell.

* Rescue – Most of us have been touched by death and loss. We've experienced the pain of separation, whether it's the death of a loved one or separation from God through our own sinful choices. But, because of Jesus, we can rejoice because sin and death will never get the last word.

Today we celebrate the birth of our Savior, knowing that was only the beginning. As Brennan Manning writes, "God entered into our world not with the crushing impact of unbearable glory, but in the way of weakness, vulnerability and need. On a wintery night in an obscure cave, the infant Jesus was a humble, naked, helpless God who allowed us to get close to him."[1] Glory to God in the highest, indeed! Give him the praise, today and everyday, that he deserves for rescuing, restoring, and reconciling us to himself!

Pause & Reflect

Spend a few moments today, amid all of the celebration, to thank God for his wonderful plan of reconciliation, restoration, and rescue.

TWENTY-SIX

Til the Season
Comes Round Again

"For everything there is a season,
a time for every activity under heaven."

ECCLESIASTES 3:1

Here we are again. Full circle from where we began. Maybe you've already started taking down your decorations. (In full disclosure, it will be several weeks before I start taking mine down. Yes, I'm one of those!) All the gifts have been unwrapped, and we begin our countdown to next Christmas anew. Three hundred and sixty-four days until we have the opportunity to celebrate this occasion again.

I'm a firm believer in the complete debrief: in examining what went well, what could have gone better, what I'd like to do again, what I'd rather never do again etc. So, how did it go? What did the last twenty-five days hold for you?

It's the day after Christmas, the perfect time to reflect and see if you celebrated differently this year, whether you made any changes that helped you be more mindful of what Christmas is really about. As the season comes to a close, do you feel like you spent most of your time managing chaos or did you fully enter into the peace and joy Christ offers?

My prayer, as you reflect over this Christmas season, is that you've experienced the power and miracle of Christ in a deeper way. As you put your Christmas decorations away, I hope that you feel a deep sense of fulfillment settle into your bones, knowing that, this time, the season didn't pass you by–Christmas truly happened *in* you.

So here are just a few questions to ask yourself to evaluate how the season went:

* Did you connect more than you consumed?

* Did you trade weariness for wonder?

* Did you choose transformation over traditions?

I hope your answer to these questions are a resounding yes, and you've discovered some new (and new meaning for old treasures) ways to receive Christ more deeply into your heart as you celebrated his birth.

Pause & Reflect

Pick one thing that you'd like to carry with you into your celebrations next Christmas and write it down in a journal or somewhere you're likely to see it next year.

TWENTY-SEVEN

You'll Find It

"This is what you're to look for: a baby wrapped
in a blanket and lying in a manger."

LUKE 2:12

As a kid, I used to snoop through my parents' closet for my Christmas gifts, until one day I was caught red-handed and red-faced, and my mom promised to return every last gift if I didn't give up my nosy ways. Her tone and expression communicated that she meant every syllable. Needless to say, that ended my exploratory missions for good!

In today's passage, the shepherds were told to look for the most unexpected thing. A baby. In a manger. They were told exactly what to look for, and fortunately for us, the Bible is still telling us what to look for.

One of my favorite passages of Scripture is Philippians 4:8, and it gives us a fantastic list of things to keep our eyes open to and our hearts fixed on. It says, "…Fix your thoughts on what is true, and honorable, and right, and pure, and lovely, and admirable. Think about things that are excellent and worthy of praise."

In today's world, this takes work. Our inboxes, TV screens, and social media feeds can be filled with the complete opposite of what this verse advises us to fill our minds with. So as the Christmas season comes to a close, let this be a reminder to carry the instructions from Philippians as well the instructions from Luke 2 with us.

Picture this: You just got a new haircut. You're feeling a little extra pep in your step, and then suddenly you start noticing all the other people who are sporting the same style. Did all of these people copy you? Probably not, your brain is now noticing something it previously ignored. By getting our new haircut, we trained our brain to subconsciously look for it everywhere.

So, what are you looking for as this Christmas season ends? Are you still looking for Jesus? You'll find him. Are you looking for stress and busy-ness? You'll find that too. Are you looking for peace among your fellow men and women and family members and also with God? Whatever your eyes are looking for, they will find. You can train your brain to focus on the good things of Philippians 4:8 and to look for the unexpected joys and surprises that God places before us regularly. Try it today.

Pause & Reflect

What are your eyes focused on right now? How can you train your
brain to focus more on the things that Philippians tells us to see?

TWENTY-EIGHT

Come, Lord Jesus

"He who is the faithful witness to all these things says,
'Yes, I am coming soon!' Amen! Come, Lord Jesus!"

REVELATION 22:20

We live in a unique time and place in history, in what William Stringfellow referred to as, "the time between the two Advents."[18] We live between what was and what is not yet, a type of anticipatory suspension between two realities.

As a teenager I went through a very definite Kenny G fangirl phase. The sweet sounds of saxophone music wafted from my bedroom at all hours. I still really love it. During the Christmas season especially, I like to listen to his holiday albums, and I find I'm drawn to the somewhat mournful sounds of his Chanukah songs. Those songs make you feel the collective weight of the history of Israel, a history filled with captivity, willful disobedience, triumph, and promised victory. The music swells with longing and desire for God to come and set all the broken things right.

It's significant that some of the final words of God to us in the Bible are an invitation to anticipation. He is coming again. Soon. This requires us to live in a certain attitude that is completely present, but also looking toward the future.

Once again, I treasure the words of the theologian Dietrich Bonhoeffer, "Through all the Advents of our life that we celebrate goes the longing for the final Advent, where it says: 'Behold, I make all things new' (Rev. 21:5). Advent is a time of waiting. Our whole life, however, is Advent–that is, a time of waiting for the ultimate, for the time when there will be a new heaven and a new earth, when all people are brothers and sisters and one rejoices in the words of the angels: 'On earth peace to those on whom God's favor rests.'"[11]

To this we say, "Come, Lord Jesus." The final words of Revelation echo in our hearts, indeed, deeply resound in our souls, as we end this season of remembrance, celebration, and significance. Acknowledging that yes, the story doesn't end here, every promise of God will be fulfilled. We have hope eternal that is as everlasting as our God.

Pause & Reflect

How does the idea of a future Advent shape your current reality? In what ways are you preparing for that day right now?

*"May God give you peace with yourselves;
may he give you good will towards all your friends,
your enemies, and your neighbors;
and may he give you grace to
give glory to God in the highest."*

CHARLES SPURGEON

Notes

1. Manning, Brennan. "Shipwrecked at the Stable." *Watch for the Light.* Plough, 2001, 184-200.

2. TerKeurst, Lysa and Joel Muddamalle. *Seeing Jesus in the Old Testament.* Proverbs 31 Ministries, 2021.

3. Nouwen, Henri. "Waiting for God." *Watch for the Light.* Plough, 2001, 27-37.

4. TerKeurst, Lysa and Joel Muddamalle. *Seeing Jesus in the Old Testament.* Proverbs 31 Ministries, 2021.

5. Spoelstra, Melissa. "A Celebration to Remember." *Joshua.* Proverbs 31 Ministries, First Five.

6. Kayla Ferris. *Pointing to the Promise.* Proverbs 31 Ministries, 2020.

7. Ross-Gotta, Loretta. "To Be Virgin." *Watch for the Light.* Plough, 2001, 96-101.

8. Moon, Kat. "Christmas Wreaths are a Classic Holiday Decoration with a Surprisingly Deep History." *Time.* 12/21/18. https://time.com/5482144/christmas-wreath-origins/ (accessed 6/11/23)

9. Leveridge, Brett. "8 Things You Should Know About the History of Nativity Scenes." *Guideposts.* https://guideposts.org/inspiring-stories/stories-of-faith-and-hope/8-things-you-should-know-about-the-history-of/ (accessed 6/22/23)

10. Weyant, Gillian. "Here is the incredible history of the Nativity Scene." Coraevans.com. https://www.coraevans.com/blog/article/history-of-the-nativity-scene-catholic-christmas (accessed 6/22/23)

11. 11 Bonhoeffer, Dietrich. "The Coming of Jesus in our Midst." *Watch for the Light.* Plough, 2001, 201-204.

12. Treisman, Rachel. "Advent calendars, explained: Where they came from and why they're everywhere now." *NPR.* 12/11/22. https://www.npr.org/2022/12/11/1141855237/advent-calendar-history-evolution (accessed 6/26/23)

13. Library of Congress. "Who Invented Electric Christmas Lights?" https://www.loc.gov/everyday-mysteries/technology/item/who-invented-electric-christmas-lights/ (accessed 6/26/23)

14. W., Audrey. "The Little-Known History of the Caroling Tradition." Arcadia Publishing. https://www.arcadiapublishing.com/Navigation/Community/Arcadia-and-THP-Blog/November-2018/The-Little-Known-History-of-the-Caroling-Tradition (accessed 6/26/23)

15. Luther, Martin. "To You Christ is Born." *Watch for the Light.* Plough, 2001, 218-224.

16. Day, Dorothy. "Room for Christ." *Watch for the Light.* Plough, 2001, 176-183.

17. Willimon, William. "The God We Hardly Knew." *Watch for the Light.* Plough, 2001, 141-149.

18. Stringfellow, William. "The Penitential Season." *Watch for the Light.* Plough, 2001, 102-106

About the Author

Erica Barthalow is a pastor's wife, former missionary, artist, and the author of *Holy Doubt* and *Praying is (not) Hard.* You can find more of her writing on relevantmagazine.com, influencemagazine.com and *Truly* magazine.

When she's not writing you can find her running with her daughter or cheering at her son's rugby matches. A midwestern girl to the core, Erica and her family live in northeast Iowa where she and her husband, Jonathan, planted Crosspoint Church and she enjoys extended winter seasons every year.

Let's Get Social!

Follow Erica for updates, art prints, giveaways, and more great content! Just scan the QR code to visit her online home:

ERICABARTHALOW.COM

INSTAGRAM: @EricaBarthalow

FACEBOOK: ericaebarthalow

PINTEREST: @EricaBarthalow

Wish You Prayed More?

Have you ever wondered why it can be so darn hard to pray? You really want to pray, you make plans to pray, you buy books about the subject, listen to podcasts and then … you still don't pray. It can leave you scratching your head wondering: *Is there something wrong with me? Why can't I just pray for heaven's sake?*

Praying is (not) Hard reveals seven surprising hang-ups that may be sabotaging your conversations with God and gives you practical steps to overcome them. If you struggle to talk with God, this book could change the way you think about prayer forever.

Through the pages of *Praying is (not) Hard* you will:

* Identify and find freedom from seven hang-ups that have kept you trapped in a frustrating cycle of inconsistent (or nonexistent) prayer.

* Discover fail proof tips and guided prompts that will have you praying before you turn the final page.

* Stop believing the lies that you're just not good at praying and nothing will ever change by flipping your perspective on prayer.

* Learn the secret that transforms distractions from a frustrating problem into the fuel for your prayers.

* Embrace the truth that God's silence doesn't indicate a lack of concern or care for you.

Get *Praying is (not) Hard* today and finally get the prayer life you've always wanted, but thought you'd never have!

Feel Alone in Your Doubts?

Does your faith in God feel fragile?

Do you wonder if there's any hope for the doubts you're experiencing?

You're not alone!

Through an honest exploration of questions like:

* Does God cause bad things to happen?

* Can he be trusted?

* Is God really good?

You'll discover how the path to a stronger, more resilient faith leads through doubt–not around it.

Get Holy Doubt today and find hope for the lonely road through doubt.

Made in United States
Orlando, FL
28 November 2024